Chia Seeus Cookbook

Simple, Healthy And Delicious Chia Seed Recipes For Everyday Life

DINGO
BOOK CLUB

"Great Books Change Life"

Table of Contents

5

Introduction

Everyone wants to be healthy and eat nutritious food. But lack of time leads us to eat takeaway food, processed meats and fast food, which does more harm to our bodies in the long run. With the growing cases of food contamination, people are becoming more aware of the food they consume and are switching to organic food items or plant-based diets to lead a healthy life. Obesity is the most common lifestyle disorder we are facing, which acts as the cause of all the other dangerous diseases like diabetes, cardiac issues, stroke, etc.

Consuming the right combination of vegetables, fruits, cereals, and spices on a regular basis would reduce the risk of these common disorders. In our busy lifestyle where we don't have time to follow traditional cooking methods or recipes, we don't usually pay attention to what our body wants and end up eating a lot of processed food and junk items. Though we try to keep ourselves healthy by planning to follow a rigid exercise routine and strict diet, we never usually implement them due to our strenuous lifestyle. One of the easiest and simplest ways to be healthy is by adding Chia Seeds to your diet. They are simple, healthy and delicious with rich nutrition benefits.

Of late, Chia seeds have become one of the favorite food items in the "stay healthy" tagline. Chia is a versatile super food and exciting ingredient that can be added easily to different food recipes. These tiny black seeds are nutrition bombs, which help maintain healthy skin, heart health, builds stronger bones and muscles, helps reverse diabetes. They are easy to digest and act as an energy booster.

In this book, we will learn about the benefits of Chia Seeds, the nutritional content they hold and how to make them a part of our regular food intake. The first chapter will talk about the history of chia seeds and its benefits while the next one will have a detailed explanation of the nutritional information of the Chia seeds and how to add it to our regular diet.

To make your life simpler, we have also compiled a wide array of recipes that use Chia seeds, so you can adapt these power bombs in your daily diet. So, let us read on and understand more.

Thanks again for purchasing this book. I hope you enjoy it!

Chapter One:
Chia Seeds and its Benefits

History of Chia Seeds

Chia seeds are edible seeds derived from the plant Salvia Hispanica grown in the deserts of Mexico by the Aztec around the 16th century. Chia seeds are aptly named so, as the word means "strength". The Aztec warriors used these tiny seeds as an energy booster. Chia seeds served as the staple food for the Aztec and Mayan population in Central Mexico. The Aztec warriors believed that these seeds would sustain an individual's survival for 24 hours without any other source of energy. They soon recognized the medicinal benefits of Chia. These seeds were used to stimulate saliva flow, to relieve joint pain and sore skin. Ground Chia seeds are still used for nutritious drinks in Argentina, Bolivia, Guatemala, Mexico, and Paraguay.

This major crop was banned after the Spanish conquest due to its close association with Aztec religion (the seeds were used in their religious rituals as offerings to God). Due to its nutritional value and stability, the commercial production of Chia seeds has resumed and has now been added to the range of healthy foods in the market.

Nutritional value

Though they are small in size, the amount of nutrients they hold is humongous. Chia seeds are an excellent source of omega-3 fatty acids, rich in antioxidants; provides fiber, iron, calcium, phosphorus, niacin, magnesium, manganese, copper, molybdenum, and zinc. Eating one ounce of chia seeds each day would satisfy 18% of daily calcium needs, 27% of daily phosphorus needs, 30% of manganese needs. They are rich in omega-3 fatty acids, potassium, copper, calcium, phosphorus and fiber as compared to flaxseeds.

The best part is chia seeds don't deteriorate and can be stored for longer periods. Also with the other benefits, these seeds also help maintain a healthy skin complexion, act as energy boosters and help reduce body weight.

Benefits of Chia Seeds

Because of the rich nutritional value they hold, there are a lot of health benefits in Chia seeds. A few of them are:

Good for Digestion

Chia seeds are rich in fiber and act as an excellent agent for digestion. It keeps the bowel related ailments like constipation away. The rich fiber content absorbs a considerable amount of water and expands in the stomach immediately, thereby making you feel 'full' faster.

Weight loss

Chia seeds top the chart when it comes to the best plant-based sources of protein. Do you want to burn extra fat and put on lean muscle? A handful of chia seeds mixed with nuts/dry fruits or soaked in water can do the magic. While exercising, it improves stamina, prolongs hydration and improves the nutrient absorption of electrolytes.

Maintains blood sugar

Chia seed consumption helps maintain healthy blood sugar levels and provides good cholesterol needed for our body. Diabetic and gluten-allergic people can safely consume these seeds, as chia seeds are entirely gluten-free.

Healthy skin and anti-aging

Due to the natural antioxidant concentration these seeds have, they play an essential role in skin repair systems and prevent premature aging. The antioxidant minerals give a natural glow to the skin.

Reduces heart diseases

The linoleic acid and the omega-3 in the chia seeds work on protecting the heart by lowering blood pressure, bad cholesterol and inflammation. Inflammation strains the blood vessels causing heart diseases; thereby consumption of chia seeds can help curb heart diseases too.

Diabetes

Recent studies revealed that these seeds could reverse diabetes when used in a planned way. Dyslipidemia and insulin resistance are the two major factors for the development of diabetes. These seeds can help prevent the above-mentioned metabolic disorders, halting diabetes and thereby reversing it. Chia seeds also reduce visceral adipose (belly fat) tissue, which is the main component of obesity. As we all know obesity disturbs the body metabolism, which leads to diabetes or other heart diseases.

Energy boosters

Consuming chia seeds before starting your exercise help in boosting the energy levels and increasing the stamina for your strict regimen.

Build stronger bones

Calcium is a vital nutrient for good bone health. One ounce of chia seeds contains 18% of the recommended daily amount of calcium.

Chapter Two: Nutritional Value of Chia Seeds

If you read any health related blogs, or other information, you will often be bombarded with the mention of Chia seeds. The trainer in the gym, the articles in health magazine, health tips you get on your mobile; all of them keep advising to include chia seeds in our diet. The reason is these seeds are rich in almost all the nutrients a human body requires.

One ounce (28 grams) of chia seeds contains 11 grams of fiber, 4 grams of protein, 9 grams of fat (out of which 5 grams are omega-3s), 18% of calcium, 30% of manganese, 30% of magnesium, 27% of phosphorus. It also includes a right amount of zinc, Vitamin B1, B2, B3, and Potassium and is a rich source of antioxidants. It has just 137 calories and 1 gram of carbs, which are easily digestible.

Fiber / Carbs

Chia is a low carb food because of its high fiber content. These seeds are 40% fiber (by weight), which is why they are referred as the best source of fiber in the world. Chia seeds absorb 10-12 times their weight in water giving it a texture of gel and allowing it to expand in your stomach. This is the reason you feel full when you consume them.

Omega 3 fatty acids

Omega 3 acid (otherwise known as Alpha Linoleic Acid (AHA)) is an essential component in body functioning. They are also called 'good fats' and play a vital role in the nervous functioning in our body. Chia seeds are naturally available sources of plant-based omega acid.

How to add Chia seeds to your diet?

Chia seeds can be eaten as whole or in grounded form. They are tiny black seeds with a nutty flavor. You can mix the seeds in water and add lime to make it into a drink or sprinkle the seeds on cereal, salads or mix them with flour while baking, etc.

Chia seeds can act as a substitute for eggs in baking. Mix two tablespoon of chia seeds with 1 cup of water and let them sit for 15-20 minutes. Beat the water well when it takes the gel form and use it instead of eggs for baking.

To ensure you have a regular intake of chia seeds, mix a spoon of these seeds in water and consume the mixture when it is soaked. While making fresh smoothies, add a tablespoon of chia seeds along with other ingredients and blend them well.

Chia seeds can be added to lemonades as a refreshing and nutritious natural cold drink.

While making your favorite desserts, you can blend chia seeds with almond milk/soy milk and add them for a rich, creamy texture. You can also sprinkle these seeds to enhance the taste of your dessert or pudding.

You can try to explore your creativity while including these seeds in your recipes and make your platter look exciting and innovative.

Chapter Three: Breakfast Recipes

Breakfast Bowl

Serves: 1

Ingredients:

For chia mixture:

- 2 tablespoons chia seeds
- 1 small banana, chopped into small pieces
- A pinch ground cinnamon
- ½ - ¾ cup almond milk
- ¼ teaspoon pure vanilla extract

For topping:

- 1 tablespoon raw buckwheat groats
- 1 tablespoons whole raw almonds, chopped
- 1 tablespoon hemp seeds
- 1 tablespoon raisins, soaked
- A pinch ground cinnamon

Method:

1. Add banana into a bowl and mash well. Add chia seeds, almond milk, cinnamon and vanilla and mix well.
2. Refrigerate for 7-8 hours.

3. Add buckwheat groats, almonds and raisins into another bowl. Pour enough water to soak. Refrigerate for 7-8 hours.
4. Drain the buckwheat mixture and rinse well. Place over the chia mixture.
5. Garnish with cinnamon and hemp seeds and serve with maple syrup (opional).

Coconut Chia Pudding

Serves: 2

Ingredients:

- ½ cup coconut milk
- ½ cup raspberries, fresh or frozen + extra to garnish
- ½ teaspoon vanilla powder or 1 teaspoon vanilla extract
- ¼ cup water
- ¼ cup chia seeds
- Sweetener of your choice to taste (optional)

Method:

1. Add water, coconut milk and raspberries into a blender and blend until smooth.
2. Add rest of the ingredients and stir.
3. Cover and chill for a few hours.
4. Serve in glasses, topped with raspberries.

Chia and Flaxseed Microwave Oatmeal

Serves: 2

Ingredients:

- 3 tablespoons rolled oats
- 1 teaspoon chia seeds
- ½ tablespoon nut butter
- Honey to taste
- ¼ cup milk of your choice
- ½ tablespoon flaxseed meal
- Ground cinnamon to taste
- Toppings of your choice like seeds, nuts, dried fruits or fresh fruits

Method:

1. Add milk, oats and chia seeds into a microwave safe bowl. Microwave on High for about 3 minutes.
2. Remove from the microwave and stir in rest of the ingredients.
3. Top with the toppings of your choice and serve.

Coconut Chia Protein Pancakes

Serves: 4

Ingredients:

- ½ cup gluten free all-purpose flour
- 6 tablespoons vanilla whey protein powder
- A large pinch sea salt
- 2 tablespoons coconut flakes
- ½ cup almond milk
- 4 tablespoons coconut flour
- 1 teaspoon baking powder
- 2 tablespoons chia seeds
- 2 eggs
- Coconut oil to fry

Method:

1. Add flour, protein powder, salt, coconut flour, coconut flakes and chia seeds into a bowl. Mix well.
2. Add eggs and almond milk and whisk until well combined.
3. Place a nonstick pan over medium heat. Add a about a teaspoon of oil. When the oil melts, pour 2-3 tablespoons of batter. In a while bubbles will appear on the top. Cook until the bottom is brown. Turn over and cook the other side too
4. Repeat with the remaining batter.
5. Serve with a topping of your choice like maple syrup, honey, berries etc.

Coconut Crunch French toast with Guava Syrup

Serves: 4

Ingredients:

For guava syrup:

- 2 cups guava puree
- 2 tablespoons palm sugar
- 2 cups water
- 2 tablespoons chia seeds

For French toast:

- 4 large eggs
- ½ cup heavy cream
- 1 tablespoon vanilla extract
- ¼ teaspoon ground nutmeg
- 2 cups coconut crunch pieces or coconut flakes
- Butter, as required
- Oil, as required
- 2 cups milk
- 4 tablespoons light brown sugar
- 1 teaspoon ground cinnamon
- 8 slices Hawaiian sweet bread or Brioche or any other sweet bread
- Confectioners' sugar to dust

Method:

1. To make guava syrup: Add all the ingredients of guava syrup into a saucepan and bring to the boil.
2. Reduce the heat to low and simmer until thick. Turn off the heat. Cover and set aside.
3. For French toast: Add eggs, cream milk and sugar into a bowl and whisk well. Add vanilla and spices and whisk until the sugar is dissolved.
4. Place coconut crunch pieces in a dish.
5. Place a large skillet over medium heat. Add about 2 tablespoons butter and 1-2 tablespoons oil. Let the pan heat.
6. Dip a bread slice in the egg mixture. Shake to drop excess egg. Dredge the slice in coconut crunch. Press lightly and place the bread in the pan. Quickly repeat the process and place 3-4 slices of bread.
7. Cook until the bottom is brown. Turn over and cook the other side too. Remove and place on a serving plate. Sprinkle confectioners' sugar on top. Drizzle warm guava syrup on top and serve.
8. Repeat the above 3 steps with the remaining bread slices.

Spinach Omelet

Serves: 1

Ingredients:

- 2 eggs
- 1 teaspoon chia seeds
- ½ cup tomatoes, chopped
- 1 teaspoon olive oil
- 1 cup baby spinach
- Salt to taste
- Pepper to taste

Method:

1. Add eggs into a bowl and beat well. Add salt and pepper and beat again.
2. Place a small nonstick pan over medium heat. Add oil. When the oil is heated, add spinach, chia seeds and tomatoes and sauté for a couple of minutes.
3. Pour egg on top and swirl the pan so that the egg spreads.
4. Cook until the eggs are set. Gently slide the omelet onto a plate and serve with toast.

Boiled, Poached or Fried Eggs

Serves: 2

Ingredients:

- 4 eggs
- Olive oil, to fry
- 2 teaspoons chia seeds
- Salt to taste
- Pepper to taste

Method:

1. Cook the eggs as per your desire (boil, poach or fry).
2. Sprinkle chia seeds, salt and pepper on top and serve.

Chia Seed Scrambled Eggs

Serves: 4

Ingredients:

- 8 eggs
- 2 teaspoons milled chia seeds
- 3 teaspoons butter
- ½ cup milk
- Salt to taste
- Pepper to taste

Method:

1. Crack the eggs into a bowl. Add chia seeds, milk, salt and pepper. Whisk well.
2. Place a saucepan over medium low heat. Add butter and the egg mixture.
3. Stir constantly until the eggs are cooked to soft and creamy consistency.
4. Serve hot.

Chapter Four: Soup Recipes

Butter Bean and Leek Soup

Serves: 3

Ingredients:

- 2 medium leeks, rinsed, white and pale green parts only, chopped
- ½ tablespoon butter
- 1 bay leaf
- ¼ red chilli, deseeded, finely chopped
- 1 can (15 ounces) butter beans, drained
- A handful parsley, chopped
- 2 teaspoons chia seeds
- ½ tablespoon olive oil
- 1 teaspoon fresh thyme, chopped
- 2 cloves garlic, finely chopped
- 2 ½ cups vegetable stock
- 1 teaspoon dried oregano
- Salt to taste
- Pepper to taste

Method:

1. Separate the rings of the leeks.

2. Place a saucepan over medium heat. Add oil and butter. When butter melts, add leeks, thyme and bay leaf and sauté until tender.
3. Add garlic and chili and sauté for a couple of minutes.
4. Add rest of the ingredients except chia seeds. Bring to the boil. Simmer for a few minutes.
5. Ladle into soup bowls. Sprinkle chia seeds on top and serve.

Tomato and Lentil Soup

Serves: 3

Ingredients:

- 1 tablespoon olive oil
- 1 stick celery, sliced
- 2 cloves garlic, finely chopped
- 6 tablespoons red lentils, rinsed
- 3 large ripe tomatoes, chopped
- 1 tablespoon milled chia seeds
- 1 carrot, chopped
- 1 medium onion, chopped
- 2 ½ cups vegetable stock
- 1 can (15 ounces) plum tomatoes
- ½ small bunch fresh basil, chopped
- Salt to taste
- Pepper to taste

Method:

1. Place a saucepan over medium heat. Add oil. When the oil is heated, add carrots, onion and celery and sauté until onions are translucent.
2. Add garlic and sauté for a few seconds until fragrant.
3. Add stock and bring to the boil. Add lentils and both the tomatoes. Let it boil.
4. Lower heat and cover with a lid. Simmer until lentils are tender.
5. Turn off heat. Add basil and chia seeds. Stir.

6. Blend with an immersion blender until smooth.
7. Add salt and pepper.
8. Ladle into soup bowls and serve.

Creamy Coconut and Carrot Soup

Serves: 2

Ingredients:

- 7 ounces canned coconut milk
- Salt to taste
- 1 teaspoon Thai yellow or red curry paste
- 6 ounces baby carrots, quartered sideways
- 1 tablespoon fresh lime juice
- 6 teaspoons chia seeds
- 1 small yellow onion, chopped
- 1 teaspoon fresh ginger, peeled, grated
- 1 clove garlic, peeled, chopped
- 1 ½ cups vegetable broth or more if required
- ¼ cup fresh cilantro sprigs
- A handful fresh cilantro, chopped

Method:

1. Place a saucepan over medium high heat. Add 2-3 tablespoons coconut milk.
2. Add onion and salt and cook until soft.
3. Add ginger, garlic and sauté for a minute or so until fragrant.
4. Add rest of the ingredients except chia seeds and stir. Bring to the boil.
5. Lower heat and cover with a lid. Simmer until carrots are tender.

6. Discard cilantro sprigs. Blend the soup with an immersion blender until smooth.
7. Add 5 teaspoons chia seeds and stir.
8. Place the saucepan back on low heat. Simmer until the chia seeds have swelled up.
9. Taste and adjust the seasonings if desired. Add more broth if the soup is very thick.
10. Ladle into soup bowls. Sprinkle cilantro and remaining chia seeds on top and serve.

Creamy Mushroom Soup

Serves: 3

Ingredients:

- ½ pound mushrooms, sliced
- 1 medium onion, chopped
- 1 small tomato, chopped
- 1 stalk celery, chopped
- 1 teaspoon olive oil
- 1 teaspoon sesame oil
- 1 clove garlic, sliced
- Salt to taste
- 1 bay leaf
- Cayenne pepper to taste
- ½ cup chia seeds
- ½ teaspoon tamari or soy sauce or to taste
- ½ cup raw cashews
- 3 cups water

Method:

1. Add cashew and water into a blender and blend until smooth.
2. Pour into a bowl. Add chia seeds and stir. Set aside for a while.
3. Place a saucepan over medium heat. Add sesame oil. When the oil is heated, add half the mushrooms and sauté for 2-3 minutes. Transfer into the bowl of cashew milk.

4. Place a saucepan over medium heat. Add olive oil. When the oil is heated, add onion, garlic and celery and sauté for a couple of minutes.
5. Add basil and tamari and stir. Add cashew milk. Bring to the boil. Turn off the heat. Cool for awhile and blend with an immersion blender until smooth.
6. Place the saucepan over medium high heat. Add remaining mushrooms, salt and cayenne pepper. Simmer for 10-15 minutes. Add tomatoes during the last 5 minutes of simmering.
7. Ladle into soup bowls and serve.

Chicken Soup

Serves: 8

Ingredients:

- 2 tablespoons quinoa
- 5 cups low fat, low sodium chicken broth
- 2 cups baby carrots, chopped into chunks
- 4 tablespoons chia seeds
- 2 small zucchinis, sliced
- 8 stalks celery, cut into bite size pieces
- 20-25 grape tomatoes
- 2 chicken breasts, cut into bite size pieces
- 4 cups fresh spinach, thinly sliced
- 2 tablespoons Japonica or Mahogany rice

For seasoning:

- 1 teaspoon dried oregano
- Pepper to taste
- ½ teaspoon ground cinnamon
- ¼ teaspoon ground cardamom
- 1 teaspoon ground coriander
- A handful fresh basil, chopped
- A handful fresh cilantro, chopped

Method:

1. Add chia seeds into a bowl. Pour 1 cup chicken broth. Set aside for a while to soak.

2. Place a saucepan over medium heat. Add 1-cup broth, quinoa and rice. Cook until tender. Add more broth if required.
3. Add chia seeds to the saucepan and cook for some more time. Turn off heat. Set aside.
4. Place a soup pot over medium heat. Add remaining broth and rest of the ingredients. Bring to the boil.
5. Lower heat and simmer until chicken is nearly tender.
6. Add the quinoa mixture and continue simmering for 5-7 minutes. Add more broth or water if the soup is very thick.
7. Add seasoning ingredients and stir.
8. Ladle into soup bowls and serve.

Chapter Five: Smoothie Recipes

Peanut Butter Banana Protein Shake

Serves: 2

Ingredients:

- 2 ripe bananas, peeled, sliced
- 1 cup almond milk, unsweetened
- 4 tablespoons peanut butter
- 2 teaspoons chia seeds
- 2 cups ice
- ¼ cup nonfat Greek yogurt
- ½ cup almonds

Method:

1. Add banana, almond milk, peanut butter, chia seeds, ice, yogurt and almonds into a blender. Blend until smooth.
2. Pour into tall glasses and serve.

Super Foods Smoothie

Serves: 2

Ingredients:

- 1 ½ cups almond milk, unsweetened
- 2/3 cup frozen strawberries
- 1 cup frozen blueberries
- 1 ripe avocado, peeled, pitted, chopped
- 1 cup spinach, torn
- 1 cup berry yogurt
- 2 tablespoons chia seeds
- 2 teaspoons flaxseeds
- 2 scoops greens superfood
- 2 scoops protein powder
- Ice cubes as required

Method:

1. Add almond milk, strawberries, blueberries, avocado, spinach, berry yogurt, chia seeds, flax seeds, greens superfood, protein powder and ice cubes into a blender.
2. Blend for 30-40 seconds or until smooth. Add more almond milk if you desire a smoothie of thinner consistency.
3. Pour into tall glasses. Garnish with slices of avocado and serve.

Tropical Green Smoothie

Serves: 2

- 1 banana, sliced, frozen
- 2 cups almond milk or coconut milk
- 2 scoops brown rice protein powder
- 2 teaspoons shredded coconut, unsweetened (optional)
- 1 cup frozen mango
- 3-4 cups baby spinach
- 1 tablespoon chia seeds

Method:

1. Add banana, milk, protein powder, mango, spinach and chia seeds into a blender and blend until smooth. Add more milk if you desire a smoothie of thinner consistency.
2. Pour into tall glasses. Garnish with shredded coconut and serve.

Healthy Strawberry Smoothie

Serves: 2

Ingredients:

- 2 cups spinach, chopped
- 10 strawberries, sliced
- 2/3 cup cooked oats
- ½ cup plain Greek yogurt
- 2 tablespoons chia seeds
- 2 cups soy milk
- Stevia to taste or maple syrup or honey
- Crushed ice

Method:

1. Retain 2 slices strawberries to garnish.
2. Add all the ingredients into a blender. Blend until smooth. Add more soy milk if you desire a smoothie of thinner consistency.
3. Pour into tall glasses. Garnish with strawberry slices and serve with crushed ice.

Blueberry and Agave Smoothie

Serve: 2

Ingredients:

- 4 cups frozen blueberries
- 3 teaspoons chia seeds
- 2 cups orange juice
- 3 teaspoons agave nectar

Method:

1. Add blueberries, chia seeds, orange juice and agave nectar into a blender.
2. Blend until smooth.
3. Pour into tall glasses and serve with crushed ice.

Green Tea & Berry

Serves: 4

Ingredients:

- 1 cup strawberries
- 1 cup blueberries
- 1 cup chilled green tea
- 4 tablespoons chia seeds
- 1 ½ cups plain lowfat Greek yogurt

Method:

1. Add strawberries, blueberries, green tea, chia seeds and yogurt into a blender.
2. Blend until smooth.
3. Pour into tall glasses and serve with crushed ice.

Snickers Smoothie

Serves: 2

Ingredients:

- 1 cup plain yogurt, unsweetened or plain kefir, unsweetened
- 2 cups almond milk, unsweetened
- Stevia or any other sweetener to taste
- 10 drops English toffee Stevia
- 2 tablespoons cocoa powder, unsweetened
- 2 heaping tablespoons peanut butter or almond butter, unsweetened
- 2 tablespoons vanilla protein powder
- 2 tablespoons chia seeds
- 1 teaspoon vanilla extract
- Ice cubes as required
- Roasted peanuts, crushed to garnish

Method:

1. Add yogurt, almond milk, Stevia, English toffee Stevia, cocoa powder, peanut butter, vanilla protein powder, chia seeds, vanilla extract and ice cubes into a blender.
2. Blend until smooth.
3. Pour into tall glasses and garnish with roasted crushed peanuts.

Super Green Coconut Detox Smoothie

Serves: 1

Ingredients:

- 1 cup spinach, torn
- ¼ cup fresh orange juice
- ¼ cup pineapple pieces
- 1 kiwifruit, peeled, chopped
- ½ cup ice
- ½ cup coconut milk
- 2 teaspoons chia seeds
- 1 medium banana, sliced
- 2 teaspoons honey
- ½ tablespoon shaved coconut (optional), to garnish

Method:

1. Add all the ingredients into a blender. Blend until smooth.
2. Pour into tall glasses. Garnish with coconut if using.

Antioxidant Smoothie

Serves:

Ingredients:

- 2 cups mixed berries of your choice
- 1 tablespoon chia seeds + extra for garnishing
- 1 cup pomegranate juice, unsweetened
- 1 cup water
- 1 cup ice cubes

Method:

1. Add berries, chia seeds, pomegranate juice water and ice cubes into a blender and blend until smooth.
2. Pour into tall glasses and serve sprinkled with chia seeds.

Raspberry Oatmeal Smoothie

Serves: 3-4

Ingredients:

- 2 bananas, peeled, sliced
- 1 cup frozen raspberries
- 1 cup old fashioned rolled oats
- ½ cup plain lowfat yogurt
- 2 tablespoons chia seeds
- 2 cups coconut water or water
- 2 tablespoons maple syrup or honey
- Crushed ice

Method:

1. Add all the ingredients into a blender. Blend until smooth. Add more coconut water if you desire a smoothie of thinner consistency.
2. Pour into tall glasses and serve with crushed ice.

Grapes, Apple, Banana and Kale Smoothie

Serves: 4

Ingredients:

- 2 cups grapes, fresh or frozen
- 2 cups kale, washed, trimmed of hard stems, chopped
- 1 medium banana, peeled, chopped
- 1 apple, cored, chopped
- 3 tablespoons chia seeds
- 1 ½ cups water

Method:

1. Add grapes, kale, banana, apple, chia seeds and water into the blender.
2. Blend until smooth.
3. Pour into tall glasses and serve with crushed ice.

Creamy Chocolate Hazelnut Shake

Serves: 4

Ingredients:

- ½ cup whole hazelnuts, soaked in water overnight, drained
- Ice cubes, as required
- 6-8 dates, pitted, soaked in water for 30 minutes, drained
- 2 tablespoons raw cacao powder or cocoa powder
- A pinch salt
- 1 ½ cups water
- 2 tablespoons chia seeds

Method:

1. Add hazelnuts, water, chia seeds, dates, cacao powder and salt into a blender.
2. Blend until smooth.
3. Add ice and blend for 10-15 seconds.
4. Pour into tall glasses and serve.

Berry Smoothie Bowl

Serves: 1

Ingredients:

- ¾ cup plain lowfat Greek yogurt
- ½ tablespoon almond butter
- ½ tablespoon chia seeds
- ½ teaspoon coconut flakes, unsweetened, to garnish
- ¾ cup frozen mixed berries of your choice
- ½ tablespoon hemp hearts
- 2 tablespoons coconut water or water
- Fresh berries to garnish

Method:

1. Add yogurt, almond butter, chia seeds, berries, hemp hearts and coconut water into a blender.
2. Blend until smooth.
3. Pour into a serving bowl. Place fresh berries and coconut flakes on top.
4. Serve at room temperature or chill and serve later.

Low Sugar Green Smoothie Bowl

Serves: 1

Ingredients:

- ½ cup coconut milk or coconut milk or unsweetened almond milk
- ½ cup spinach
- 1 ½ cups assorted kale like curly and lacinato, discard hard ribs and stem, torn.
- ½ ripe avocado, peeled, pitted, chopped
- ½ small banana, frozen
- 1 Brazil nut
- ½ teaspoon ground cinnamon
- ¼ teaspoon ground ginger
- ½ date, pitted
- 1 teaspoon moringa powder
- A pinch salt
- ½ scoop protein powder or collagen powder
- 2 teaspoons almond butter
- ½ teaspoon turmeric powder
- Ice cubes as required
- Kiwi slices to serve
- 1 teaspoon chia seeds to serve
- 1 teaspoon coconut flakes, unsweetened to serve

Method:

1. Add all the ingredients except kiwi slices, chia seeds and coconut flakes into a blender.
2. Blend until smooth.
3. Pour into a bowl. Sprinkle chia seeds and coconut flakes on top. Garnish with kiwi slices and serve.

Chapter Six: Snack Recipes

Devilled Chia Eggs

Serves: 3 (2 halves each)

Ingredients:

- 3 eggs, hard boiled, peeled, halved lengthwise
- A large pinch ground mustard
- ½ tablespoon chia seeds
- 1 ½ tablespoons mayonnaise
- Salt to taste
- Paprika to taste
- 1 teaspoon parsley, chopped

Method:

1. Carefully remove the yolks from the egg halves and place in a bowl. Mash with a fork.
2. Add mayonnaise, parsley, chia seeds, mustard and salt and mix well.
3. Fill this mixture in the cavity of the egg whites.
4. Sprinkle paprika on top. Chill for an hour and serve.

Quinoa Chia Seed Protein Bars

Serves: 6

Ingredients:

- ¼ cup dry quinoa
- 1 tablespoon ground flax seeds
- A pinch Himalayan salt
- ½ teaspoon ground cardamom
- 2 tablespoons honey
- ¼ cup almond butter
- ¼ cup chia seeds
- ½ cup rolled oats
- ¼ cup almonds, chopped
- 2 tablespoons brown rice syrup

Method:

1. Add almond butter, honey and brown rice syrup into a microwave safe bowl. Microwave on High for 40-50 seconds or until it melts. Mix well.
2. Add rest of the ingredients into a bowl and stir.
3. Pour the almond butter mixture into it. Mix well. You may have to use your hands to mix.
4. Line a baking dish with parchment paper. Transfer the mixture into the baking dish. Spread it evenly with a spatula. Place the dish in the middle rack of a preheated oven.
5. Bake at 350 F for around 15 minutes.
6. Cool for 10-15 minutes. Remove the baked bar along with the parchment paper and cool on a wire rack.
7. Cut into 6 equal squares and serve.

Cheese Balls

Serves: 6 (3 balls each)

Ingredients:

- 4 ounces plain almond milk cream cheese
- 4 ounces goat's cheese
- ¼ teaspoon garlic, minced
- A handful fresh cilantro, finely chopped
- ¼ cup roasted, salted almonds, chopped
- 4 teaspoons chia seeds
- Pepper powder to taste
- Salt to taste

Method:

1. Add goat's cheese and cream cheese into a bowl.
2. Beat with an electric mixer on medium speed until smooth.
3. Add cilantro, salt, pepper and garlic and mix. Place the bowl in the freezer for 15 minutes.
4. Add nuts into the food processor bowl and pulse until fine. Transfer into a bowl. Add chia seeds and mix.
5. Divide the mixture into 18 equal portions and shape into balls.
6. Dredge the balls in the nut –chia seed mixture. Cover and chill until use.
7. Serve with a dip of your choice.

Caramelized Hemp and Chia Seed Popcorn

Serves: 4

Ingredients:

- 4 cups popped unsalted or low sodium popcorn
- 1 tablespoon coconut oil, melted
- 1 ½ tablespoons hemp seeds or hemp hearts
- A large pinch ground nutmeg
- 1 ½ tablespoons pure maple syrup
- 1 ½ tablespoons coconut sugar or brown sugar
- 1 ½ tablespoons chia seeds
- A large pinch salt

Method:

1. Place a sheet of parchment paper on a baking sheet. Set aside.
2. Add popcorn into a large bowl. Mix together maple syrup and coconut oil in a bowl and pour over the popcorn. Toss well.
3. Add coconut sugar, half the chia seeds, and half the hemp seeds, salt and nutmeg into a bowl and mix well. Sprinkle over the popcorn and toss.
4. Spread the popcorn on the prepared baking sheet. Spread and press lightly into a single layer.
5. Sprinkle remaining chia seeds and hemp seeds on top.
6. Bake in a preheated oven at 275 F for around 20 minutes.
7. Remove from the oven and cool completely. Break the popcorn and add into an airtight container.

8. Serve as required.

Chapter Seven: Salad Recipes

Power Salad with Lemon Chia Seed Dressing

Serves: 2

Ingredients:

For salad:

- 2 cups packed spinach, torn
- ½ cup cooked quinoa
- ¼ cup almonds, chopped
- ½ cup red cabbage, chopped
- 1 medium sweet potato, peeled, cubed, roasted
- 7.5 ounces canned chickpeas, rinsed, drained
- 1 medium Gala or Fuji apple, cored, diced
- 1 medium avocado, peeled, pitted, sliced

For lemon chia seed dressing:

- 2 tablespoons olive oil
- 1 tablespoon golden or white balsamic vinegar
- 1 teaspoon chia seeds
- Salt to taste
- Freshly ground pepper to taste
- 1 tablespoon fresh lemon juice

- 1 teaspoon honey or agave nectar

Method:

1. Add all the ingredients of the salad into a bowl and toss well.
2. To make dressing: Add all the ingredients of the dressing into a small jar. Fasten the lid and shake the jar vigorously until the mixture is well combined.
3. Pour over the salad. Toss well and serve.

Chia Chicken and Avocado Salad with Honey Mustard Dressing

Serves: 4

Ingredients:

- 4 chicken breasts, skinless, boneless, sliced into thin long strips
- 4 tablespoons olive oil
- 4 cups mixed baby salad leaves
- 2 large avocados, peeled, pitted, sliced
- ½ cup pine nuts, toasted
- Salt to taste
- Pepper to taste
- 4 cups spinach, chopped
- 2 cups cherry tomatoes, halved
- 1 cup feta cheese, crumbled
- 4 tablespoons whole chia seeds

For honey mustard dressing:

- 4 tablespoons extra virgin olive oil
- 2 teaspoons English mustard
- Salt to taste
- Pepper to taste
- 2 tablespoons freshly squeezed lemon juice
- 2 teaspoons honey

Method:

1. To make dressing: Add all the ingredients of the dressing into a small jar. Fasten the lid and shake the jar vigorously until the mixture is well combined.
2. To make salad: Sprinkle salt and pepper over the chicken strips.
3. Place a skillet over medium heat. Add 2 tablespoons oil. When the oil is heated, add chicken strips and cook until brown and tender. Stir occasionally. Remove with a slotted spoon and set aside on a plate that is lined with paper towels.
4. Repeat the above step with remaining oil and chicken.
5. Add spinach and salad leaves into a large bowl. Mix well.
6. Add rest of the salad ingredients and toss well.
7. Drizzle the dressing on top. Toss well and serve.

Spicy Chorizo and Goat's Cheese Chia Salad with Herb Dressing

Serves: 2

Ingredients:

- ½ cup goat's cheese
- ½ tablespoon olive oil
- ½ cup cherry tomatoes, halved
- 3 cups baby salad leaves
- 1 tablespoon whole chia seeds
- Pepper to taste
- ½ chorizo sausage (about 4 ounces)
- ¼ cup pickled beetroot, drained, cubed
- 2 tablespoons hazelnuts, toasted

For herb dressing:

- 3 tablespoons extra virgin olive oil
- 2 tablespoons parsley, chopped
- Salt to taste
- Pepper to taste
- 1 tablespoon red wine vinegar
- ½ teaspoon honey

Method:

1. To make dressing: Add all the ingredients of the dressing into a small jar. Fasten the lid and shake the jar vigorously until the mixture is well combined.

2. To make salad: Place goat's cheese on a baking sheet. Sprinkle pepper on top.
3. Broil for a few minutes until the cheese melts.
4. Place a skillet over medium heat. Add oil. When the oil is heated, add sausage and sauté until the juices are released.
5. Remove the sausage with a slotted spoon and place on your cutting board. Cut into half-moon shaped slices.
6. Place the skillet back on heat. Add cherry tomatoes and cook for a couple of minutes. Turn off the heat.
7. To assemble: Place the salad leaves on a serving platter (otherwise take 2 individual serving plates and divide equally the ingredients). Place beetroot cubes over it. Sprinkle hazelnuts and chia seeds.
8. Lay the sausage slices over it followed by tomatoes and finally goat's cheese. Pour dressing on top and serve right away.

Quinoa Salad with Feta and Chia Seeds

Serves: 2-3

Ingredients:

- 2 cups water
- ¼ teaspoon salt
- 1 cup quinoa, rinsed
- 2 tablespoon chia seeds, lightly toasted
- 3 tablespoons kalamata olives, pitted, chopped
- A handful fresh mint or oregano, chopped
- 1 ½ tablespoons olive oil
- ¾ cup cherry tomatoes, halved
- 1 small red onion, chopped
- 2 ounces feta cheese, crumbled
- ½ tablespoon apple cider vinegar or sherry vinegar

Method:

1. Place a saucepan over medium heat. Add water and bring to the boil.
2. Add quinoa and bring to the boil.
3. Lower heat and cover with a lid. Simmer until quinoa is cooked and all the liquid in the saucepan dries.
4. When done, fluff with a fork.
5. Add toasted chia seeds, olives, tomatoes, onion, mint, vinegar, oil and feta and mix well.
6. Taste and adjust the seasoning if necessary.
7. Serve.

Chia Seed and Cucumber Salad

Serves: 2

Ingredients:

- 2 Persian cucumbers, trimmed, halved lengthwise, deseeded, sliced
- ½ tablespoon apple cider vinegar
- A pinch granulated sugar
- 2 teaspoons red onion, finely minced (optional)
- 2 tablespoons Greek yogurt
- 1 tablespoon chia seeds
- Salt to taste

Method:

1. Add cucumber into a bowl. Add rest of the ingredients into the bowl and mix well.
2. Refrigerate for 4-6 hours.
3. Taste and adjust the seasoning if required.

Quinoa Salad with Chipotle Chia Dressing

Serves: 2-3

Ingredients:

- 2 cups water
- ¼ teaspoon salt
- 1 cup quinoa, rinsed
- 1 red bell pepper, chopped
- 1 yellow bell pepper, chopped
- 1 small cucumber, chopped

For chipotle chia dressing:

- ¼ cup fresh or store bought orange juice
- 1 tablespoon olive oil
- 1 teaspoon agave nectar
- 1 clove garlic, minced
- Salt to taste
- 1 ½ tablespoons fresh lime juice
- ½ tablespoon chipotle chiles in adobo sauce, chopped
- ½ tablespoon chia seeds
- ¼ teaspoon ground cumin

Method:

1. To make dressing: Add all the ingredients of the dressing into a small jar. Fasten the lid and shake the jar vigorously until the mixture is well combined.

Place the jar in the refrigerator and chill until the chia swells.

2. When the chia seeds swells, place a saucepan over medium heat. Add water and bring to the boil.
3. Add quinoa and bring to the boil.
4. Lower heat and cover with a lid. Simmer until quinoa is cooked and all the liquid in the saucepan dries. When done, fluff with a fork. Transfer into a bowl. Let it cool for awhile.
5. Transfer into a large bowl. Add bell peppers and cucumber and mix. Pour dressing on top. Mix well and serve.

Chapter Eight: Accompaniments Recipes

Cheesy Bread

Serves: 12

Ingredients:

- 12 eggs
- 1 ½ cups kefir
- 6 cups almond flour
- 3 cups raw cheese, shredded
- 1 cup + 2 tablespoons water
- 1 ½ teaspoons sea salt
- 1 ½ tablespoons pepper
- 2 ¼ cups chia seeds

Method:

1. Add eggs, kefir, salt, pepper and water into a bowl and whisk well.
2. Stir in the flour, chia seeds and cheese and mix well.
3. Pour the batter into a loaf pan that is greased with a little oil or butter.

4. Bake in a preheated oven at 350 F for 40-50 minutes or until done.
5. When done, remove from the oven and cool.
6. Slice and serve.

Nutty Spiced Pumpkin Crackers

Serves: 12

Ingredients:

- 3 cups almonds, sliced
- 4 tablespoons chia seeds
- 3 teaspoons pumpkin pie spice mix
- ½ cup pumpkin puree
- 2 tablespoons coconut oil
- ½ cup golden flaxseed meal
- 3 tablespoons honey
- 1 teaspoon salt
- 2 large egg whites

Method:

1. Place all the ingredients into the food processor bowl. Pulse until the almonds are chopped into smaller pieces and slowly the mixture will form into dough.
2. Place the dough in between 2 sheets of parchment paper. Roll with a rolling pin into a rectangle with a thickness of 2 mm. carefully peel off the top parchment sheet.
3. Lift the bottom parchment paper carefully (along with the rolled dough) and place on a large baking sheet. Make small cuts all over the dough.
4. Bake in a preheated oven at 325 F for 20-30 minutes until light golden brown in color.

5. Remove from the oven and cool completely. Break into pieces and transfer into an airtight container.

Chia Tortillas / Wraps

Serves: 15-16 wraps

Ingredients:

- 1 cup chia seeds
- 1 cup ground flaxseeds
- 2/3 cup raw buckwheat groats
- ½ cup sorghum flour
- 4 cups warm water
- 4 tablespoons olive oil
- 2 teaspoons salt

Method:

1. Line 4 baking sheets with parchment paper and set aside.
2. Add chia seeds into a blender and blend into a fine powder. Transfer into a large bowl and add warm water. Whisk simultaneously as you add the water. Set aside for 2-3 minutes. No longer than this.
3. Add buckwheat groats into the blender and blend into a fine powder. Transfer into the bowl of chia seeds powder.
4. Add flaxseed, salt, olive oil and sorghum into the bowl and mix well.
5. Pour about 1/3 cup of the prepared batter on one side of the baking sheet. Similarly pour 1/3 cup of batter on the other side of the baking sheet.

6. Take a parchment paper and place over the batter. Press in a circular manner so that the batter spreads until it is ¼ inch in thickness.

7. Bake in a preheated oven at 350 F for 10-12 minutes. Flip sides half way through baking. When done, remove from the oven and cool for a minute. Remove the tortilla and place on a cooling rack. Do not keep for longer than a minute on the parchment paper; or else it will stick to it.

8. Repeat steps 5-7 to make the remaining tortillas.

Blackberry Chia Jam

Makes: 2 cups

Ingredients:

- 2 cups blackberries
- 3 tablespoons lemon juice
- 4 tablespoons chia seeds
- 2 medium nectarine or peach, peeled, cored, cubed
- 4 tablespoons honey

Method:

1. Add blackberries, nectarine and lemon juice into a pan. Place the pan over medium heat.
2. In a while the blackberries and nectarine will begin to release its juices. Mash with a potato masher.
3. Simmer until slightly thick. Add honey and chia seeds and cook for a couple of minutes.
4. Turn off the heat. Let it cool for awhile.
5. Transfer into a glass jar. Fasten the lid. Refrigerate until use.
6. It can store for 2 weeks in the refrigerator.

Chia seed and Strawberry Jam

Makes: 2/3 cup

Ingredients:

- 4 ounces fresh strawberries, chopped
- 1 tablespoon chia seeds
- 2 tablespoons sugar or erythritol, powdered
- 2 tablespoons water

Method:

1. Add strawberries into a small pan. Place the pan over medium heat.
2. Add sugar or erythritol and stir. In a while the strawberries will begin to release its juices. Mash the strawberries with a potato masher.
3. Simmer until slightly thick. Add chia seeds and cook for a couple of minutes.
4. Turn off the heat. Let it cool for awhile.
5. Transfer into a glass jar. Fasten the lid. Refrigerate until use.
6. It can store for 2 weeks in the refrigerator.

Chapter Nine: Main Course Recipes

Cornmeal & Chia Seed Crusted Tilapia

Serves: 2

Ingredients:

- 2 tilapia fillets, boneless, pat dried
- 2 teaspoons low fat mayonnaise
- ½ teaspoon chia seeds
- Olive oil cooking spray
- Kosher salt to taste
- Pepper to taste
- 6 tablespoons cornmeal
- ¼ teaspoon garlic powder

Method:

1. Mix together cornmeal, chia seeds, salt, pepper and garlic powder on a plate. Set aside.
2. Place a cooking rack on a baking sheet. Spray the rack with cooking spray.
3. Season the fish with salt and pepper. Spread a teaspoon of mayonnaise on each fish.

4. Carefully dredge the mayonnaise side of the fish in the cornmeal mixture. Press into the mixture well.
5. Place the fish on the rack with the coated side facing up.
6. Bake in a preheated oven at 400 F for 15-20 minutes until the fish is cooked through and the top is crunchy.

Californian Avocado Toasts

Serves: 4

Ingredients:

- 4 slices whole wheat bread, toasted
- 2 tablespoons salted cashews
- 1 teaspoon chia seeds
- 1 Californian avocado, peeled, pitted, sliced
- 4 tablespoons craisins

Method:

1. Place the toasted bread slices on a serving platter.
2. Place avocado slices over it. Sprinkle craisins and chia seeds. Place cashews over it and serve.

Linguine Al Limone with Grilled Chia Chicken

Serves: 6

Ingredients:

- 1/3 cup white chia seeds
- 1 ½ pounds ground chicken
- ½ cup red onion, coarsely grated or minced
- 4 ½ tablespoons extra-virgin olive oil
- 2 teaspoons fresh oregano, minced or 1 teaspoon dried oregano
- 2 teaspoons salt or to taste
- ¾ teaspoon red pepper flakes
- ½ cup half and half
- 3 tablespoons fresh basil, thinly sliced (optional)
- ¾ cup purified water
- 1 cup + 2 tablespoons rolled oats (old fashioned oats)
- ¾ cup Parmigiano – Reggiano cheese
- 1/3 cup flat leaf parsley, finely chopped
- 3 cloves garlic, peeled, minced
- 1 ½ teaspoons freshly ground pepper or to taste
- 18 ounces whole grain linguine
- Juice of 1 ½ lemons
- Zest of 1 ½ lemons, grated

Method:

1. Add water and chia seeds into a bowl. Stir and set aside for 20 minutes.
2. Add chicken, chia mixture, oats, 1/3-cup cheese, parsley, 3 tablespoons oil, oregano, 1 ½ teaspoons salt, red pepper flakes and ¾ cup black pepper into a large bowl. Mix well.
3. Divide the mixture into 30 equal portions and shape into balls.
4. Grill the balls in a preheated grill for about 15 minutes until brown on the outside and cooked inside. Turn the balls every 3-4 minutes.
5. You can also place the balls on a baking sheet and bake at 475 F for about 20 minutes.
6. Prepare the linguine following the instructions on the package. Retain about 1-½ cups of the cooked water.
7. Add about a cup of the retained water into a saucepan. Add half and half and stir. Place the saucepan over high heat. Bring to the boil.
8. Add remaining cheese, salt, pepper and lemon juice and mix well. Add the pasta and toss until well combined.
9. Divide the pasta among 4 bowls. Place meatballs on top. Garnish with basil and lemon zest. Serve right away.

Lentils with Chia Seeds

Serves: 6

Ingredients:

- 3 tablespoons olive oil
- 1 ½ teaspoons cumin seeds
- 1 ½ teaspoons garlic, minced
- 1 ½ teaspoons turmeric powder
- 3 cups red lentils, rinsed
- 1 teaspoon salt or to taste
- Cooked brown rice to serve
- 2 medium onions, chopped
- ¼ teaspoon ground cardamom
- 3 tablespoons fresh ginger, minced
- 1 fresh jalapeño, sliced
- 1 ½ cans tomatoes
- 5-6 cups vegetable stock
- 2 tablespoons chia seeds
- ½ cup fresh cilantro, chopped

Method:

1. Place a large saucepan over medium heat. Add oil. When the oil is heated, add onions and sauté until light brown.
2. Add cumin seeds and sauté for a minute.
3. Add garlic and cardamom and sauté until fragrant.
4. Add water, turmeric, ginger, jalapeño, stock, tomatoes and lentils and bring to the boil.

5. Lower heat and cover with a lid. Simmer until the lentils are tender.
6. Add chia seeds, salt, and cilantro. Stir and serve over brown rice.

Chicken Red Curry

Serves: 6

Ingredients:

- 1 ½ pounds chicken thighs, skinless, boneless, chopped into chunks
- 1 ½ tablespoons vegetable oil
- 5 cloves garlic, thinly sliced
- 1 large red bell pepper, thinly sliced
- 8- scallions, thinly sliced
- 1 head broccoli, cut into florets
- Juice of 1 ½ lemons
- Zest of 1 ½ lemons, grated
- 4-5 tablespoons light soy sauce
- 1 ½ tablespoons palm sugar
- 22 ounces full fat coconut milk
- 1 red chili, thinly sliced
- 3 tablespoons red curry paste
- 1 cup chicken stock
- 1 ½ tablespoons fish sauce
- 3 tablespoons whole chia seeds
- Cooked rice to serve

Method:

1. Place a wok over high heat. Add oil. When the oil is heated, add chili and garlic and sauté for a few seconds until fragrant.

2. Stir in the curry paste. Add about ½ cup of coconut milk and mix well. Cook for a couple of minutes.
3. Add chicken and sauté for 5 minutes. Add bell pepper and broccoli and sauté for a few minutes until crisp as well as tender. Stir in the scallions.
4. After 2-3 minutes, add lime juice, lime zest, stock, soy sauce, fish sauce, coconut milk and palm sugar and mix well.
5. Simmer for 3-4 minutes.
6. Turn off heat and chia seeds. Mix well.
7. Serve over cooked rice.

Chapter Ten: Dessert Recipes

Peach Cobbler

Serves: 4-5

Ingredients:

- 1 ½ cup peaches, peeled, chopped
- ¼ teaspoon coconut oil
- A pinch sea salt
- ¼ cup butter or ghee
- 1 ½ tablespoons chia seeds
- ½ tablespoon coconut vinegar
- 1 cup almond flour
- ¼ teaspoon baking soda
- 6 tablespoons honey
- 2 drops almond extract
- 4 tablespoons warm water

Method:

1. Grease a small baking dish with coconut oil.
2. Add peaches into the dish. Spread it evenly.

3. Add almond flour, baking soda and salt into a bowl and mix well.
4. Add butter, almond extract and honey into a bowl and mix well. Pour into the bowl of almond flour. Mix well.
5. Add chia seeds and hot water into a bowl and mix well. Set aside for 5 minutes. Stir and transfer into the almond flour mixture. Mix well. Add vinegar and mix well.
6. Pour the mixture on the peaches. Spread it evenly.
7. Bake in a preheated oven at 350 F for 30-45 minutes until golden brown.

Healthy Sundae

Serves: 12

Ingredients:

- 2 ripe bananas, sliced, frozen
- 2/3 cup pineapple, chopped
- 2/3 cup kiwi, chopped
- Any other fruit of your choice
- 4 strawberries, chopped
- 4 dates, pitted, chopped
- ¼ cup nuts of your choice
- 1/3 cup boiling water
- 1/4 cup almond milk
- ¼ teaspoon ground ginger
- ½ tablespoon almond butter, unsweetened
- 1 cup granola of your choice
- 2 tablespoons chia seeds

Method:

1. Soak dates in boiling water for at least 45 minutes.
2. Add dates and ginger along with water into a blender and blend into a smooth sauce and keep it aside.
3. Clean the blender and blend together the frozen bananas, almond butter and almond milk. Transfer into 12 freezer safe dessert bowls and freeze until done.

4. Remove from the freezer and sprinkle pineapple, kiwi, strawberry pieces and any other fruit you are using on top.
5. Sprinkle granola, nuts and chia seeds. Pour date sauce on top and serve.

Fruit Salad

Serves: 6

Ingredients:

- 3 mangoes, peeled, pitted, diced
- ¾ cup blackberries
- 3 kiwifruits, peeled, diced
- 10 strawberries, sliced
- 4 tablespoons lime juice
- 2 tablespoons raw honey
- 3 tablespoons chia seeds

Method:

1. Add honey into a bowl and place the bowl in a bigger bowl with warm water in it. In a while, the honey will melt.
2. Add lime juice and chia seeds and stir.
3. Add all the fruits into a bowl and toss well. Pour dressing on top. Toss well.
4. Chill and serve.

Chia Seed Wafer Cookie

Serves:

Ingredients:

- 1 ½ cups chia seeds, lightly toasted
- 2 egg whites
- 1 cup agave nectar
- 1 cup flour
- ½ teaspoon baking powder
- ½ cup whipped butter, softened
- 1 cup coconut sugar
- 1 teaspoon vanilla extract
- ½ teaspoon salt

Method:

1. Add all the ingredients into a bowl and mix well.
2. Line a baking sheet with parchment paper.
3. Drop tablespoonful of batter on the baking sheet. Leave a gap of about 1-½ inches between 2 cookies.
4. Bake in a preheated oven at 375 F for 6-8 minutes.
5. Remove from the oven and cool for 2 minutes. Remove the cookies from the parchment paper and place on a cooling rack.
6. Transfer into an airtight container.

Tropical Coconut Mango Chia Pudding

Serves: 3

Ingredients:

For chia pudding:

- 1 ¼ cups plain coconut milk, chilled
- 1 teaspoon vanilla extract
- ½ tablespoon grated coconut
- A pinch powdered cardamom
- 6 tablespoons chia seeds
- 2 teaspoons honey or maple syrup
- ¼ teaspoon ground cinnamon

For coconut mango puree:

- 1 medium mango, peeled, pitted, chopped
- 4 teaspoons grated coconut
- 3-4 teaspoons honey

For topping:

- 1 tablespoon shaved coconut, toasted

Method:

1. To make chia pudding: Add coconut milk, vanilla, coconut, chia seeds, honey and spices into a bowl. Mix well.
2. Cover and refrigerate for 4-8 hours.

3. To make coconut mango puree: Add mango, grated coconut and honey into a blender and blend until smooth.
4. Pour into a bowl and chill for a couple of hours.
5. To assemble: Take 3 glasses. Spoon in about a tablespoon of mango puree alternating with chia seed pudding in each glass. Make layers in this manner until all the puree and chia seeds are used.
6. Sprinkle coconut shaving on top.
7. Chill until use.

Conclusion

With that, we have come to an end of this book. I hope you found the book informative and interesting.

You can use this book as a simple guide to understand the health benefits of chia seeds and try to use them in your regular diet to ensure you stay healthy. Since these seeds are readily available in the local market as well as on online shopping sites, you can start adding them to your food recipes. The recipes in this book will ensure you consume ample quantities of this nutritious superfood. Don't restrict your creativity and get more innovative with your recipes.

Thank You!

Before you go, we'd like to say thank you for purchasing our book and congratulations for reading until the end.

If you found the book valuable, can you recommend it to others? One way to do that is to post a review on Amazon. Click Here to leave a review for this book on Amazon!

If you want to leave a private feedback, please email your feedback to: feedback@dingopublishing.com

Your feedback is important to us. We value and appreciate receiving your compliments or suggestions. Your feedback will help us continue to improve our books.

Thank you and good luck!

P/S: Don't forget to grab your free bonus and join Dingo Book Club today!

More books from us

Visit our bookstore at: http://www.dingopublishing.com

Below is some of our favorite books:

THE TOP 99 DELICIOUS RECIPES TO
FIGHT CANCER AND RESTORE YOUR HEALTH

ANTI-CANCER
Diet

Olivia Green

WHAT YOU NEED TO KNOW ABOUT FUCOIDAN & AHCC
UNDERSTAND THEIR BENEFITS AND SIDE EFFECTS FOR CANCER TREATMENT

ANTI-CANCER
Nutrients
FUCOIDAN & AHCC

Olivia Green

RAMEN
NOODLES COOKBOOK
The Top 50 Delicious
Ramen Recipes To Cook At Home

LINDA NGUYEN

THAI
Simple Cookbook
QUICK AND EASY AUTHENTIC THAI
RECIPES TO MAKE AT HOME

LINDA LY

HIIT

BURN FAT AND BUILD LEAN BODY FASTER WITH
HIGH INTENSITY INTERVAL TRAINING

JOSHUA KING

INTERMITTENT FASTING

THE ULTIMATE GUIDE TO BURN FAT
AND BUILD LEAN BODY

JONATHAN SMITH

JAPANESE ETIQUETTE

The Essential Guide to Japanese
Traditions, Customs, and Etiquette

VINCENT MILLER

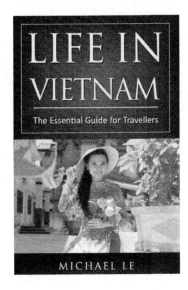

LIFE IN VIETNAM

The Essential Guide for Travellers

MICHAEL LE

Bonus chapters

'Anti-Inflammatory Diet For Beginner'
by Jonathan Smith.

Introduction

These days, everywhere you go and every website you visit, you are going to find discussions or adverts about this or that diet program. Diets that can help you lose weight, diets that can cure cancer, and even diets that promise to increase your bank account. Some of these diets work; others are a waste of your time, energy, and financial resources. The anti-inflammatory diet is nothing like these fad diets. This revolutionary diet draws upon a simple scientific and biographical logic guaranteed to work for you regardless of your circumstances.

The anti-inflammatory diet has many innate benefits including lowering your risk of heart diseases, protecting the bones, helping you maintain a healthy weight, and increasing your body's ability to absorb nutrients from the foods you eat and the drugs you take.

This book is a comprehensive guide that shall impart upon you everything you need to know about the anti-inflammatory diet. Let's begin.

Chapter 1: Introduction to the Anti-Inflammatory Diet

To make this book easy to read and follow, we will start by understanding inflammation and the anti-inflammatory diet.

In its simplest terms, an anti-inflammatory diet simply refers to a collection of foods that have the ability to fight off chronic inflammation in your body.

So what exactly is chronic inflammation?

Well, before we discuss that, let's start by understanding what inflammation is first.

So what is inflammation?

Inflammation is simply a term used to refer to your body's response to infection, injuries, imbalance, or irritation with the response being swelling, soreness, heat, or loss of body function. It is the body's first line of defence against bacteria, viruses and various other ailments. The goal is to 'quarantine' the area and bring about healing/relief. This is the good inflammation, as it is helpful to your body. It is often referred to as acute inflammation. However, there are times when the inflammatory process might not work as expected resulting to a cascade of activities that could ultimately result to cell and tissue damage especially if it takes place over a prolonged period. This is what's referred to as chronic inflammation. This type of inflammation has nothing to do with injuries; it is not as a result of an injury or anything related to bacteria, virus or any other microbe. And unlike acute inflammation that comes with soreness, pain, heat and swelling, chronic inflammation comes with another set of symptoms some of which include diarrhoea, skin outbreaks, congestion, dry eyes, headaches, loss of joint function and many others. This inflammation is what you need to fight using an anti-inflammatory diet because if it is not addressed early, it might result to a number of various chronic health complications that we will discuss in a while.

So how exactly does this chronic inflammation develop that would actually require a diet to undo? Here is how:

It all starts in the gut. The gut essentially has a large semi-porous lining, which tends to fluctuate depending on various chemicals that it comes into contact with. For instance, if exposed to cortisol, a hormone that is high when you are stressed, the lining becomes more permeable. The lining also becomes a lot more permeable depending on the changing levels of thyroid hormones. This increased permeability increases the likelihood of viruses, bacteria, yeast, toxins and various digested foods passing through the intestines to get into the bloodstream, a phenomenon referred to as leaky gut syndrome (LGS). The thing is, if this (the intestinal lining becomes damaged repetitively), the microvilli in the gut start getting crippled such that they cannot do their job well i.e. processing and using nutrients with some enzymes that are effective for proper digestion. This essentially makes your digestive system weaker a phenomenon that results to poor absorption of nutrients. If foreign substances find their way into the bloodstream through the wrong channels, this results to an immune response that could result to inflammation and allergic reactions. This form of inflammation can bring about different harmful complications. What's worse is that as inflammation increases, the body keeps on producing more white blood cells to fight off the foreign bodies that have found their way into the bloodstream. This can go on for a long time resulting to malfunctioning of different organs, nerves, joints, muscles, and connective tissues.

Chronic inflammation is harmful to your body and your brain. Let me explain more of this:

Your body is responsible for supplying glucose to your brain so that your brain can perform optimally. When you eat too much inflammation-causing foods, your body slows down its process of transporting glucose to the brain since it concentrates on fighting off the inflammation. Your brain then keeps asking the body for glucose since it is not getting its fill. This effect causes you to crave sugary and pro-inflammatory foods. Inflammation can also result to abnormal levels of water retention along with other problems that contribute to stubborn weight gain. This just worsens the condition and causes your inflammation to worsen. Unfortunately, majorities of dieters focused on weight loss only focus on reducing calories and fatty foods but pay very little attention to how eating pro-inflammatory foods may be contributing to an inability to lose weight quickly.

If inflammation persists, it can bring about a wide array of health complications some of which include:

- Obesity and chronic weight gain

- Lupus

- Arthritis

- Cancer

- Diabetes

- Celiac disease

- Crohn's disease

- Heart disease

So how exactly does inflammation lead to disease? That's what we will discuss next.

How Inflammation Could Lead to Diseases

It is possible to have a disease-free body, but only if you can manage to keep your body balanced. Diseases develop only when something upsets the equilibrium (balance) of the body. An abnormal composition of blood and nymph is a typical example of such imbalance. These two are responsible for supplying the tissues with nutrients and carrying away eliminated toxins, metabolic by-products and wastes from the liver and kidneys. When you consume unhealthy meals, it may affect the balance of blood and nymph in the body and lead to inadequate supply of nutrients and thus, the body would be unable to give adequate support to kidney and liver function. The consequence of this is that it exposes the body to the risks of several diseases and inflammatory conditions, which I mentioned earlier.

Food Allergies, Food Intolerance, and the Anti-Inflammatory Diet

Food allergies happen when your immune system reacts to the proteins in certain foods. Your immune system releases histamines that may cause production of throat mucous, runny nose, watery eyes, and in severe cases, diarrhea, hives, and anaphylaxis.

Your immune system's reaction to food allergies is to trigger inflammatory responses because when a food causes allergic reaction, it stimulates the production of antibodies that bind to the foods and may cross-react with the normal tissues in your body.

One of the highpoints of the anti-inflammatory diet is that it calls for the elimination of foods that promote allergies and intolerance.

How the Anti-Inflammatory Diet Works

To cure and stop incessant inflammation, you must eliminate the irritation and infection, and correct hormonal imbalance by eating specific foods while avoiding others. This would help stop the destruction of cells and hyperactive response of your immune system. When on an anti-inflammatory diet, most of the foods you shall be eating have powerful antioxidants that can help prevent and eliminate symptoms of inflammation.

For instance, anti-inflammatory foods such as avocados contain Glutathione, a powerful antioxidant. Radishes contain Indol-3-Carbinol (13C), which increases the flow of blood to injured areas. Pomegranates have polyphenols that stop the enzyme reactions the body uses to trigger inflammation. Shiitake Mushrooms are high in polyphenols that protect the liver cells from damage. Ginger has hormones that help ease inflammation pain.

We will discuss more on the foods you should eat and those you should avoid later.

In the next chapter, we shall look at the basic rules of the anti-inflammatory diet as well as how to get the best out of the diet program.

Chapter 2:
Basic Rules of the Anti-Inflammatory Diet

As is the case with any diet, the anti-inflammatory diet has basic rules but as you are about to find out, these rules are very easy to follow and straightforward: no extreme rules that would leave you cravings-crazy and running back to a poor eating style after a few days.

When following this diet, there are about 11 rules you should follow:

1st: You Must Eat at Least 25 Grams of Fiber Daily

These should be whole grain fibrous foods such as oatmeal and barley, vegetables such as eggplant, onions, and okra, and fruits like blueberries and bananas. These fiber-rich foods have naturally occurring phytonutrients that help fight inflammation.

2nd: Eat at Least Nine Servings of Fruits and Vegetables Daily

A serving of fruit refers to half a cup of fruits while a serving of vegetable refers to a cup of leafy green vegetables. You could also add some herbs and spices such as ginger, cinnamon, and turmeric, foods that have strong anti-inflammatory and antioxidant properties.

3rd: Eat at Least Four Servings of Crucifers and Alliums Every Week

Crucifers refer to vegetables such as Brussels sprouts, Broccoli, mustard greens, Cabbage, and Cauliflower. Alliums refer to onions, garlic, scallions, and leek. These foods have strong anti-inflammatory properties and may even lower risks of cancer. You should eat at least four servings of these every day, and at least one clove of garlic daily.

4th: Consume Only 10% of Saturated Fat Daily

The average daily recommended calories for adults is about 2,000 calories every day. This means you have to limit your daily saturated fat caloric intake to no more than 200 calories. If you consume less than 2,000 calories daily, you have to reduce accordingly.

Saturated fats include foods like hydrogenated and partially hydrogenated oils, pork, desserts and baked goods, sausages, fried chicken and full fat diary. Saturated fats often contain toxic compounds that promote inflammation, which is why you need to eliminate these foods from your diet.

5th: Eat a Lot of Omega-3 Fatty Acid Rich Foods

Omega-3 fatty acids rich foods such as walnuts, kidney, navy and soybeans, flaxseed, sardines, salmon, herring, oysters, mackerel and anchovies are an essential part of this diet thanks to their strong anti-inflammatory properties.

6th: Eat Fish Thrice Weekly

It is important that you eat cold-water fish and low-fat fish at least three times a week because fishes are rich sources of healthy fats and can be great substitutes for saturated and unhealthy fats.

7th: Use Healthier Oils

The fact that you have to reduce your intake of some types of fat does not mean you should stop consuming all fats. You only need to reduce or even eliminate the consumption of unhealthy ones and limit your intake of healthy ones like expeller pressed canola, sunflower and safflower oil, and virgin olive oil. These oils have anti-oxidant properties that help detoxify the body.

8th: Eat Healthy Snacks at Least Twice Daily

Unlike in most diets, in this diet, you get to eat snacks as long as it is healthy. You can snack on healthy foods such Greek Yoghurt, almonds, celery sticks, pistachios, and carrots.

9th: Reduce Consumption of Processed Foods and Refined Sugars

Reducing your intake of artificial sweeteners and refined sugars can help alleviate insulin resistance and lower risks of blood pressure. It may also help reduce uric acid levels in your body. Having too much uric acid in your body may lead to gout, kidney stones, and even cancer. A high level of uric acid in the body is usually because of poor kidney function. Overloading your kidneys with pro-inflammatory foods may reduce kidney function and subsequently lead to excessive uric acid levels in the body.

Reducing your consumption of refined sugars and foods high in sodium can help reduce inflammation caused by excess uric acid within the body.

10th: Reduce Consumption of Trans Fat

Studies by the FDA reveal that foods high in trans-fat have higher levels of C-reactive protein, a biomarker for inflammation in the body. Foods like cookies and crackers, margarines, and any products with partially or fully hydrogenated oils are some of the foods with high trans-fat content.

11th: Use Fruits and Spices to Sweeten Your Meals

Instead of using sugar and harmful ingredients to sweeten your meals, use fruits that can act as natural sweeteners such as berries, apples, apricot, cinnamon, turmeric, ginger, sage, cloves, thyme, and rosemary.

Now that we have laid down the rules, the next thing we will do is to put what we've learnt into perspective i.e. what foods you should eat and what you should avoid. The next chapter has a comprehensive list of foods to consume and foods to avoid while on this diet. Consider printing out the chapter so you can use it as a reference each time you need to cook or make shopping decisions. If you do, it will not be long before you get used to the diet and can quickly decipher foods which foods you should and should not buy.

Anti-Inflammatory Diet for Beginner

By: Jonathan Smith

Find out more at:

http://dingopublishing.com/book/anti-inflammatory-diet-beginners/

Thanks again for purchasing this book.

We hope you enjoy it

Don't forget to claim your free bonus:

Visit this link below to claim your bonus now:

http://dingopublishing.com/heath-freebonus/

Printed in Great Britain
by Amazon

10791877R00068